PEPPERS

A COOKBOOK

BY ROBERT BERKLEY · PHOTOGRAPHS BY ERIC JACOBSON

DESIGN BY LESLEY EHLERS

A FIRESIDE BOOK
PUBLISHED BY SIMON & SCHUSTER INC.

NEW YORK   LONDON   TORONTO   SYDNEY   TOKYO   SINGAPORE

A RUNNING HEADS BOOK

FIRESIDE
Simon & Schuster Building
Rockefeller Center
1230 Avenue of the Americas
New York, New York 10020

FIRESIDE and colophon are registered trademarks of Simon & Schuster Inc.

PEPPERS: A COOKBOOK
was conceived and produced by
Running Heads Incorporated
55 West 21 Street
New York, New York 10010

Editor: Linda Greer
Production Manager: Peter McCulloch
Managing Editor: Jill Hamilton

3 5 7 9 10 8 6 4 2

Library of Congress Cataloging in Publication Data

Berkley, Robert.
Peppers : a cookbook / by Robert Berkley : photographs by Eric
Jacobson.
p.   cm.
"A Fireside book."
ISBN 0-671-74598-0
1. Cookery (Peppers)   2. Peppers.   I. Title.
TX803.P46B47   1992
6416′5643—dc20   91-3508
CIP

Typeset by Trufont Typographers, Inc.
Color separations by Hong Kong Scanner Craft Company, Ltd.
Printed and bound in Singapore by Tien Wah Press (Pte.) Ltd.

For Rebecca.

AUTHOR'S ACKNOWLEDGMENTS

I would like to extend my special thanks and gratitude to the following people, whose help and support and contributions to this project are most appreciated: Nancy and Sam Freitag, Mildred and William Raucher, Michelle Hauser, Aubrey Mkanda, all of my friends at Delta 88 restaurant in New York City, the staffs of Balducci's, Dean and DeLuca and the Jefferson Market, Chris Hansen, and Steve Cioffi.

Special thanks also to Marta Hallett, Ellen Milionis, Linda Greer, Lindsey Crittenden, Jill Hamilton, Peter McCulloch, Enid Rivera and the rest at Running Heads, as well as to Karen Holden, Mary Kapp, Clare Wellnitz, and all the others at Simon & Schuster.

PHOTOGRAPHER'S AND DESIGNER'S ACKNOWLEDGMENTS

We would like to thank the following people for their support during this project: the Jacobson and Ehlers families, Judy Devine, Dexter Samuel, Jill Bock, Beth Farb, Michele Cohen, Kim Kelling, Robin Van Loben Sëls, Doug Hay, Maggie Jones, Jeffrey Stern and Myriam Zwierzinska.

Thanks also to the many people and companies who loaned us their beautiful tablewares: Ceramic Stiles, Williams-Sonoma, Pottery Barn, Piece Meals table linens by Carole Shiber, Douglas Benoit of Ben Designs, Laura Beck at Platypus, Kaija at Ceramica, and Pauline Kelley and Lorena Sita at Zona.

Very special thanks to Keith and Chuck in the produce department at Publix Supermarket, Fort Myers, FL, for sending us their gorgeous peppers.

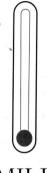

MILD

Scoville units
0

WARM

Scoville units
1–1,500

MEDIUM

Scoville units
1,500–5,000

HOT

Scoville units
5,000–300,000

♦◄◄◄◄◄◄ INTRODUCTION ♦►►►►►◄

One of the earliest plants to be domesticated in the Americas, the pepper originated in South America and spread north and east, to Central and North America and the Caribbean. When Christopher Columbus traveled to the West Indies in the late fifteenth century, he returned to Europe with a number of New World agricultural products, among them peppers. Thanks in part to Columbus, peppers are grown today on nearly every continent. The passion for the unusually flavorful and often hot pepper is so strong that many countries and cultures have adopted it as an integral part of their culinary identity. It would be impossible to imagine what Mexican food, for example, would be like without its earthy sauces made from dried peppers, or its piquant fresh chili salsas. And what would Korean food be without its ever-present, pungent kimchis, or Indian food without its spicy vindaloos?

Capsicums, as they are formally known in botanical Latin, or "peppers" as they are more commonly known, grow in hundreds of forms. A common means of categorizing the many types is according to their level of "heat," or spiciness. The heat in a pepper is produced by a chemical called capsaicin, a substance so potent that it retains its strength through almost any processing method. The Scoville test is a standard means of rating the intensity of heat produced by a pepper. Named for its developer, Wilbur L. Scoville, the test yields a numerical value, based on capsaicin concentration, on a scale of 0 (bell peppers, sweet Italian peppers) to 300,000 (habaneros) or more. The higher the number, the hotter the pepper. The Scoville test can only indicate an exact number for any one pepper; peppers within a particular variety can vary widely in capsaicin content. With this in mind, we have divided the book into four chapters, from mild through hot, according to the Scoville unit range of each pepper. A pepper guide on pages 12 to 15 identifies the peppers found in this book (which are some of the most widely available) and their approximate value in Scoville units. Most of the recipes in this book include directions for removing the seeds from the pepper before using it. Seeds interfere with the texture of the dish, and may also contain a good bit of capsaicin. The ribs, however, contain the highest concentration of capsaicin of any part of the pepper, and should be removed any time less heat is desired. It is wise to wear gloves while handling the hottest peppers—capsaicin has been known to cause pain even to the skin—and you should be particularly careful not to touch your eyes or other sensitive areas.

After much experimenting with peppers it became clear to me that it is their distinct flavors, rather than their varying degrees of heat, that truly defines them. Therefore, when selecting recipes for each pepper, I focused on those that emphasize each type's flavor rather than showcasing its heat potency. As a result, just because a pepper appears in the hot section, a fiery recipe does not necessarily accompany it, though some *are* downright scorching. Habanero Hot Sauce (page 110), for example, which is made up almost entirely of habanero peppers, is very, very hot. Cold Shrimp with Cayenne Mayonnaise (page 96), on the other hand, which has only a bit of cayenne in the dipping sauce, needn't be terribly hot—the intensity can be adjusted simply by using more or less pepper.

There are several remedies for the effects of eating a pepper that is too hot for you, something that is usually discovered when it is too late. (Eventually, you can build up a tolerance to the heat of peppers, and will be able to eat hotter and hotter chilies without having to resort to these cures.) Many people recommend drinking tomato juice or eating a fresh lemon or lime, the theory being that the acid counteracts the alkalinity of the capsaicin. Some people won't begin eating hot peppers without a pitcher of cold water handy, though this is not the best idea: The capsaicin, which is an oil, does not mix with the water but is instead distributed to more parts of the mouth. More useful solutions include drinking milk (rinsing the mouth with it as you sip) or eating rice or bread, which absorb the capsaicin. My own favorite retaliation against attack by hot chili pepper is to simply eat another. And if *that* doesn't work, eat another one.

When buying fresh peppers always select those that are firm, never deflated or wrinkled. Peppers usually show their ripeness by turning from green to red or orangish; the riper the pepper, the more mature the flavor. Many varieties, however, can be found in a wide range of colors, from pale chartreuse to intense, dark green, and from light yellow through orange and bright red. There are even purple bell peppers on the market; though these mysteriously turn green when cooked, they are quite striking when used raw.

There are several ways to prepare a pepper before using it in a recipe. Many dishes call for roasting and peeling the pepper. Some peppers can be found in the markets already in this state (often called pimientos), but the variety is limited and they are seldom as good as those you make at home. The most commonly roasted peppers are the red and yellow bells; others are certainly roastable, but the bell is most suited for this particular process because of its thick flesh and sweet flavor. There are two methods of roasting a pepper that are equally acceptable. The first is to place the pepper in a very hot oven in a shallow baking pan or an ovenproof skillet. Leave it there, turning occasionally, for about 30 minutes or until the skin has begun to wrinkle, darken and recede from the flesh. Remove the pepper from the oven, place it in a bowl and cover tightly. Allow the pepper to cool, also about 30 minutes. With clean hands, carefully remove the skin from the pepper, saving the flavorful liquids that emerge. Do not try to save time by holding the pepper under running water while you peel it, as much of the valuable flavor will wash off. Discard the skin, stem and seeds. Roasted peppers can be chopped and held in their natural juices and a little olive oil in the refrigerator for several weeks.

Another way to roast a pepper is to put it directly over or under an open flame. This can be done on a grill or a camp fire, over a burner or under a broiler. The close contact with the heat source will scorch the outside of the pepper, charring the skin. If attended to, turning the pepper frequently so just the skin is burnt, the flesh of the pepper will survive the process unharmed. Complete the process the same way as the oven-roasting method, by covering, cooling and peeling. The back of a small knife might help remove the charred skin.

Roasting peppers other than the bells requires a little more of a watchful eye because their flesh is not as dense. Once finished, roasted peppers can be eaten plain, as a garnish or as an accompaniment to grilled chicken or fish. They can be pureed and made into a soup, as in Roasted Yellow Bell Pepper Soup (page 22), or they can be sliced into strips and added to a salad, such as Roasted Red Bell Pepper and Green Bean Salad (page 26). Or they can be combined with other ingredients and become the central figure in a dish such as Marinated Bell Pepper and Mushroom Relish (page 34).

Pickling is another popular way to prepare peppers. It is also a good way to preserve them and to mellow the heat from a hot chili a bit. The flavor is, naturally, affected by whatever you are pickling the peppers in and with. Traditional pickling techniques call for vinegar, sugar and salt, but garlic, onions, seeds (such as coriander and caraway) and herbs (such as dill) can all add new dimensions to the flavors of the peppers as they cure in their jars. There may be some color loss in the peppers, but they can remain pickled for several months or even years if kept in a cool place away from direct light. My favorite pickled-pepper recipe can be found in this book—Habanero Hot Sauce (page 110), which is simply pickled minced peppers. The flavor is distinct and powerfully hot, but when added in modest doses to a plate of rice and beans or a dish of plain canned corn it interacts in a sublime manner.

Drying is a third common method of preparing peppers. Dried peppers are available in most markets in most cities, and a wide variety are available through mail-order sources, but they are very easy to make at home and are a luxurious addition to any pantry. Drying peppers is also a foolproof method of preserving them. Be sure to start with peppers that are at least partly red (ripe), and use those types with thin flesh (bells and jalapeños, for example, do not dry well). If you live where it is dry and sunny, tie the stems of the peppers together and hang them in the sun to ripen and dry for several days. One good indoor method is to put your peppers into a commercial food dehydrator; another is to dry them in a 200°F oven for 6 to 8 hours. Store dried peppers in a dry place and use them whole, crushed, or seeded and then ground into a fine powder.

While both roasted and pickled peppers are often eaten on their own without any further preparation, dried peppers, which contain the essence of the fresh without the substance, must be reconstituted in some way before they are consumed. There are several ways to do this. One is to soak whole dried peppers in hot water or plain tea for about 20 minutes. The skin can then usually be removed pretty easily (especially from larger varieties), if desired. Discard the stem and seeds and proceed with the recipe. Another way to rehydrate a dried pepper is by simply adding it to whatever it is you are cooking: Whole dried peppers added to a simmering liquid or stew will impart a spicy flavor, but are generally removed after cooking and not eaten; crushed or ground peppers can be added to almost any dish while it cooks and can even be used as a table condiment, like salt and black pepper, sprinkled on moist foods. Dried peppers can add an extra layer of flavor to almost any dish, if used moderately and treated like a spice.

Depending on where you are, a pepper's name may vary. In New York markets an Anaheim and a New Mexico pepper are the same, though the Anaheim is actually just one variety of New Mexico pepper. On one occasion I asked for rocotillo peppers and turned up empty, but I looked myself and found them under the name aji (elsewhere a generic term for any hot pepper). Habaneros are sometimes called Scotch bonnets, and there is often confusion about anchos and poblanos, which are the names usually assigned to the fresh (poblano) and dried (ancho) versions of the same pepper. In shopping for peppers, whether fresh or dried, be flexible and be prepared to try a variety you're not familiar with—fresh peppers are highly seasonal, and the availability of both fresh and dried frequently follows regional patterns, depending on what ethnic groups predominate.

There are no rules for substituting a pepper for one that is unavailable. Let common sense be your guide: Choose a pepper with a similar flavor and texture to stand in for the original if you wish to retain the fundamental character of the dish. For instance, substitute one sweet bell pepper for another, one sharp cayenne for several piquin chilies, or two biting serranos for a Thai. It's also possible to alter the nature of a recipe by, for instance, using the comparatively mild rocotillo in place of the incendiary habanero. There are hundreds of pepper flavors in the world—don't be afraid to try them all!

Bell *0 Scoville units*
Available fresh (green, red, yellow, orange and purple).

Sweet Italian *0 Scoville units*
Available fresh (usually light green, sometimes orange to red).

12

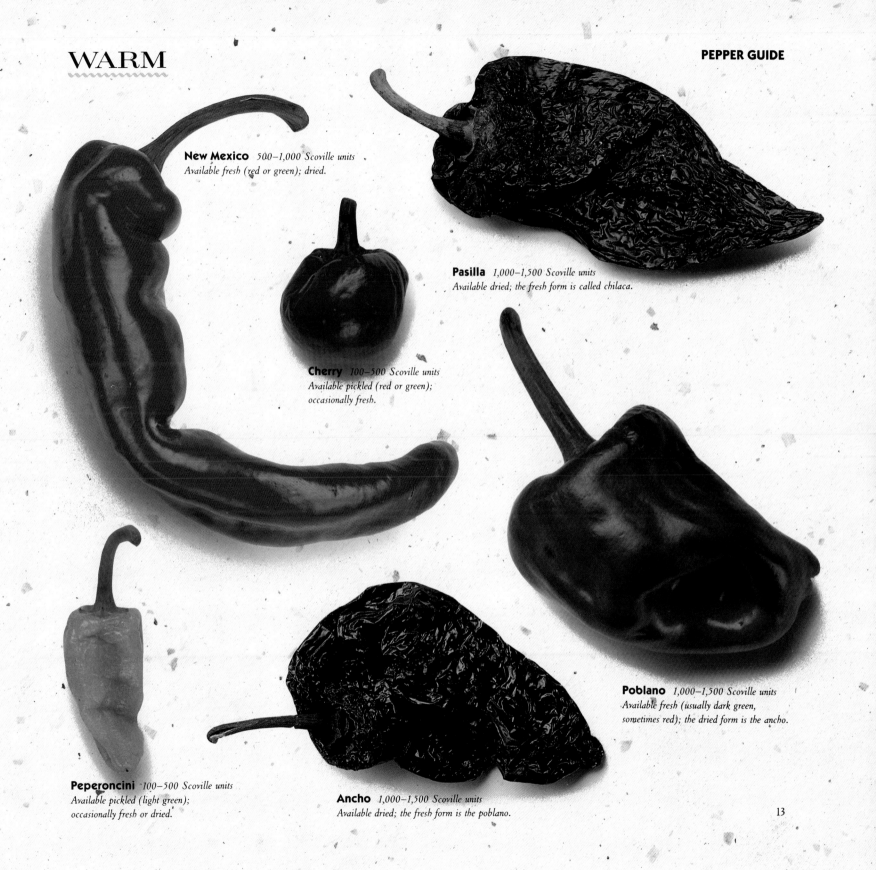

WARM

New Mexico *500–1,000 Scoville units*
Available fresh (red or green); dried.

Pasilla *1,000–1,500 Scoville units*
Available dried; the fresh form is called chilaca.

Cherry *100–500 Scoville units*
Available pickled (red or green);
occasionally fresh.

Poblano *1,000–1,500 Scoville units*
Available fresh (usually dark green,
sometimes red); the dried form is the ancho.

Peperoncini *100–500 Scoville units*
Available pickled (light green);
occasionally fresh or dried.

Ancho *1,000–1,500 Scoville units*
Available dried; the fresh form is the poblano.

MEDIUM

Jalapeno *2,500 5,000 Scoville units
Available fresh (usually green, sometimes red);
pickled; the smoked form is the chipotle.*

Rocotillo *1,500–2,500 Scoville units
Available fresh (light green and yellow
through orange and red).*

Chipotle *2,500–5,000 Scoville units
Available smoked then either dried or canned;
the fresh form is the jalapeño.*

Wax *5,000–10,000 Scoville units
Available fresh (light yellow).*

Guajillo *2,500–5,000 Scoville units
Available dried.*

14

Cayenne *30,000–50,000 Scoville units*
Available dried; occasionally fresh (red or green).

Piquin *30,000–50,000 Scoville units*
Available dried; occasionally fresh or pickled (green).

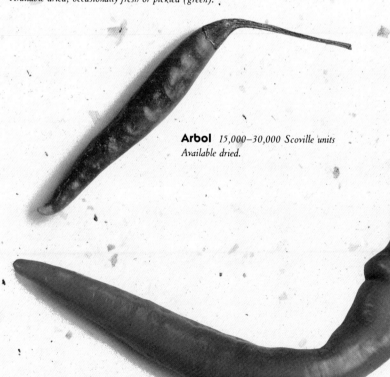

Arbol *15,000–30,000 Scoville units*
Available dried.

Habanero *100,000–300,000 Scoville units*
Available fresh (light green and yellow through orange and red).

Thai *50,000–100,000 Scoville units*
Available fresh (red or green).

Serrano *10,000–23,000 Scoville units*
Available fresh (usually red, sometimes green or yellow).

MILD

Green Bell Pepper and Bacon Frittata

6 slices bacon
1 green pepper, seeded and coarsely
chopped
2–3 scallions, chopped
8 eggs
¼ cup milk
salt and pepper

• Preheat oven to 450°.
• Cook the bacon in an ovenproof skillet until crisp. Remove the bacon from the pan and place on paper towels, leaving the fat in the pan.
• Add the chopped pepper and scallions to the skillet and sauté over medium heat until softened. Lower the heat, crumble the bacon and add to the skillet.
• Break the eggs into a bowl and beat briefly with the milk. Pour into the skillet and mix quickly with the pepper, scallions and bacon. Cook over low heat until the frittata is firm most of the way through. Add salt and pepper to taste. Place in the oven for 3 to 5 minutes to finish cooking. Cut into wedges to serve.

Serves 4.
Preparation time: 30 minutes.

Sweet Italian Pepper and Onion Bread

1 tablespoon sugar
1 package active dry yeast
3½ cups all-purpose flour
1 tablespoon salt
2 sweet Italian peppers, seeded and diced
1 small onion, diced
2–3 tablespoons olive oil

- Dissolve sugar and yeast in ¼ cup warm water. Set aside until mixture is foamy, about 5 to 10 minutes.
- Combine flour and salt in a large bowl. Add ¾ cup warm water to the flour mixture and combine well. Add yeast mixture and continue mixing until all liquid is incorporated. Knead on a floured surface for several minutes, until dough becomes elastic. Add diced peppers and onion, and work into the dough until evenly distributed. Form the dough into a smooth ball.
- Generously coat the inside of a bowl with olive oil. Place the dough in the oiled bowl and turn it so that it becomes coated with the oil. Cover with a damp cloth and set aside in a warm place to rise, about 1½ to 2 hours.
- When the dough is doubled in size, punch it down and knead it for a minute or 2. Form the dough into 2 balls and dust with a little flour. Cut an X or a few slashes in the top of each ball (about ½ inch deep) to keep the bread from cracking when it bakes. Place the dough on a baking sheet, cover with a cloth, and set aside in a warm place to rise for another 45 minutes.
- Preheat oven to 400°.
- After the second rising, remove the cloth and bake the bread for 30 to 40 minutes, until it sounds hollow when you tap on the crust.

Makes 2 small loaves.
Preparation time: 4 hours.

Roasted Yellow Bell Pepper Soup

6 yellow bell peppers
1 quart chicken stock
salt and pepper

• Preheat oven to 400°.
• Place the peppers in a shallow baking pan and roast for 20 to 30 minutes, turning occasionally, until the skin has darkened and separated and the peppers have wilted.
• Put the peppers and any liquid that has accumulated in a bowl; cover tightly and set aside. When the peppers have cooled, peel and seed them (do not do this under running water).
• Puree the peppers and any accumulated liquids in a blender or food processor and pour into a 2-quart saucepan. Add the chicken stock. Bring to a boil, add salt and pepper to taste and serve hot.

Serves 4.
Preparation time: 1 hour.

Scallop and Yellow Bell Pepper Skewers

vegetable oil
16 large sea scallops
1 large yellow bell pepper, seeded and
cut into 1-inch squares
4 skewers
1 orange, quartered

• Preheat grill to high following manufacturer's instructions. (Or preheat broiler if no grill is available.) Brush the surface of the grill with a bit of vegetable oil to prevent sticking.
• Arrange 4 scallops and 4 pieces of pepper on each skewer.
• Place the skewers on the grill and squeeze an orange quarter over them. Cook for about 5 minutes (just until the scallops lose their translucence), turning occasionally. Squeeze more orange juice over the skewers with each turn.

Serves 2 to 4.
Preparation time: 20 minutes.

Roasted Red Bell Pepper and Green Bean Salad

2 red bell peppers
½ pound green beans, ends trimmed
½ cup canned large lima beans, rinsed,
or frozen, thawed
3 tablespoons red wine vinegar
6 tablespoons extra-virgin olive oil
½ teaspoon ground cumin
salt and pepper

- Preheat oven to 400°.
- Place peppers in a shallow pan and roast for 20 to 30 minutes, turning occasionally, until the skin of the peppers darkens and separates. Put peppers and any accumulated juices into a bowl and cover tightly. Allow to cool.
- While peppers are cooling, bring a medium-sized pot of water to a rapid boil. Place the green beans in the boiling water and cook for 1 minute. Remove to a colander and put under cold running water until they are thoroughly cooled. Julienne the beans and set aside.
- When peppers have cooled, peel and seed them. (Do not peel under running water.) Cut peppers into strips and return them to the bowl with their juices. Add the green beans and lima beans.
- In a separate bowl, whisk together the vinegar, oil, cumin, and salt and pepper to taste. Pour over salad and mix thoroughly.

Serves 4.
Preparation time: 1 hour.

Sweet Italian Peppers with Chicken and Pignoli Stuffing

8 sweet Italian peppers
½ pound ground chicken
2 ounces pignoli nuts
1 egg white
4 tablespoons heavy cream
½ teaspoon chopped fresh tarragon or
¼ teaspoon dried
salt and pepper
vegetable oil

- Preheat oven to 350°.
- Remove stems and seeds from peppers and set aside.
- Combine chicken, pignoli nuts, egg white, cream and tarragon in a bowl. Add salt and pepper to taste and mix thoroughly.
- Stuff the chicken mixture evenly into the peppers and place in a lightly oiled baking pan. Bake in the oven for 30 minutes or until peppers are tender.

Serves 4.
Preparation time: 45 minutes.

Bell Pepper Confetti Pizza

1 package active dry yeast
2 tablespoons sugar
2 cups all-purpose flour
salt
6–10 tablespoons vegetable oil
1 green bell pepper, seeded and diced
1 red bell pepper, seeded and diced
1 yellow bell pepper, seeded and diced
2 scallions, chopped

• Combine the yeast, sugar and ¼ cup warm water in a bowl. When the yeast is very foamy (about 5 to 10 minutes), stir in the flour, a pinch of salt and 2 tablespoons of oil. Knead the dough with your hands to form a smooth ball and return it to the bowl. Cover with a damp cloth and set aside in a warm place to rise for about 30 minutes.

• While the dough is rising, heat 2 tablespoons of oil in a skillet over medium-low heat. Add the peppers and scallions and sauté until tender, about 10 minutes. Set pan with mixture aside.

• After the dough has risen, divide it into 4 equal pieces. Lightly flour your work surface and roll each piece of dough into a 6-inch circle.

• Heat 2 tablespoons of oil in an 8-inch skillet over medium-high heat. Place a piece of rolled-out dough in the hot oil and fry until golden. Turn and fry for another minute. Remove to paper towels to drain. Repeat with the other 3 pieces of dough, adding more oil as necessary. Keep fried dough pieces warm.

• Place the pan containing the pepper mixture over medium heat and rewarm the mixture. Spoon evenly in the centers of the 4 pieces of dough.

Serves 4.
Preparation time: 1 hour 15 minutes.

Veal Rolls with Sweet Italian Pepper Filling

3 tablespoons vegetable oil
2 sweet Italian peppers, seeded and diced
3 scallions, chopped
¼ pound fresh or frozen spinach (thawed and drained), coarsely chopped
salt and pepper
4 4-ounce veal cutlets, pounded very thin

- Preheat oven to 450°.
- Heat 1 tablespoon of oil in a skillet over medium heat. Add the peppers and scallions and sauté until wilted, about 5 minutes. Add the spinach and cook for a few more seconds, just until the spinach is warmed through. Remove from heat, add salt and pepper to taste and allow to cool.
- When the pepper mixture is cool enough to handle, spread it evenly over the cutlets. Roll the cutlets and tie each with unbleached string.
- Heat the remaining oil in an ovenproof skillet. Add the veal rolls and brown well on all sides. Place in the oven to finish cooking, about 5 minutes. To serve, cut off string and slice rolls on an angle.

Serves 2.
Preparation time: 45 minutes.

Marinated Bell Pepper and Mushroom Relish

1 yellow bell pepper
1 red bell pepper
¼ pound mushrooms, quartered
2 bay leaves
½ cup cider vinegar
2 tablespoons sugar
2 scallions, coarsely chopped, for
garnish (optional)

- Preheat oven to 400°.
- Place peppers in a shallow baking pan and roast in the oven, turning frequently, until the skins darken and separate, about 20 to 30 minutes. Remove from oven, place in a bowl, cover tightly and allow to cool. Peel and seed the peppers, reserving any accumulated juices in the bowl. (Do not peel under running water.) Cut the peppers into strips and return to bowl.
- Add the mushrooms, bay leaves, vinegar and sugar; mix well. Refrigerate, covered, at least overnight (or up to a week). Garnish with chopped scallions if desired.

Serves 6.
Preparation time: 1 hour, plus marinating time.

Pickled Sweet Italian Peppers, Carrots and Cauliflower

4 carrots, peeled and sliced into rounds
½ head cauliflower, cut into florets
8 sweet Italian peppers, seeded and cut
into large rings
1–1½ quarts rice vinegar
¼ cup sugar
2 tablespoons coriander seeds

• Place the carrots and cauliflower into a steamer basket or colander in a large pot. Add a small amount of water; cover and steam just until the vegetables start to become tender, but are still fairly firm. Run carrots and cauliflower under cold water until they are cool. Drain, add the peppers and place all in a 2-quart jar.

• Combine 1 quart vinegar, sugar and coriander seeds, and pour over the vegetables in the jar. Add extra vinegar if the vegetables are not covered. Cover and refrigerate for at least 2 days before serving. Will keep in the refrigerator for several weeks.

Makes 2 quarts.
Preparation time: 30 minutes, plus pickling time.

Red Bell Pepper and Tomato Juice

1 large, ripe beefsteak tomato, cored
1 large red bell pepper, seeded and
coarsely chopped

• Cut the tomato in half and squeeze out the seeds. Place in a blender with the pepper and puree. Strain and serve chilled.

Serves 2.
Preparation time: 10 minutes, plus chilling time.

WARM

Peperoncini and Roast Beef Hash

2 tablespoons vegetable oil
1 small onion, diced
6 dried peperoncini peppers, coarsely
broken, or 6 pickled, seeded and
chopped
2 small new potatoes, cut into ¼-inch
cubes (skin optional)
¼ pound roast beef, cut into ¼-inch
cubes
½ cup chicken or beef broth
salt and pepper

• Heat vegetable oil in a large skillet over medium-high heat. Add the onion and peppers and sauté until onion is wilted, about 3 minutes. Add the potatoes and cook, stirring occasionally, until lightly browned, about 10 minutes.
• Mix in the roast beef and sauté for a minute. Add the broth and salt and pepper to taste, being careful not to oversalt if the broth is already salty. Lower heat to medium and cook, stirring occasionally, until the liquid is evaporated and the potatoes are tender, about 15 minutes.

Serves 2.
Preparation time: 30 minutes.

Salmon with New Mexico Pepper and Lime

1 tablespoon vegetable oil
1 fresh red or green New Mexico
pepper, seeded and diced
juice of 6 limes
2 cups clam juice
4 6-ounce pieces salmon fillet
¼ cup heavy cream

- Heat the oil in a large skillet. Add the pepper and sauté just until softened, 2 to 3 minutes. Add the lime juice and bring to a boil. Reduce until only 1 or 2 tablespoons of liquid remain.
- Add the clam juice and bring to a boil. Reduce to a low simmer. Place the salmon pieces in the pan, flesh side up, and poach until firm but not overcooked, about 10 minutes. Remove salmon to a plate and refrigerate.
- Slowly stir the cream into the poaching liquid and continue to simmer over very low heat. When the sauce begins to thicken, spoon 2 tablespoons over the cooling salmon in the refrigerator. Repeat this every few minutes until all of the sauce has been added to the fish. The sauce may be somewhat thin when you begin, but will be quite thick by the last few spoonfuls. Serve chilled.

Serves 4.
Preparation time: 1 hour.

Cold Potato and Pasilla Pepper Soup

1 tablespoon vegetable oil
1 medium-sized onion, chopped
2 large Idaho potatoes, peeled and sliced
2 cups chicken broth
2 dried pasilla peppers, soaked in hot
water for 30 minutes, seeded and
chopped
salt and pepper

• Heat the oil in a medium-sized saucepan over medium heat. Add the onion and sauté until translucent, about 5 minutes. Add the potatoes and continue cooking for a few minutes. Add the chicken broth and bring to a boil. Reduce heat and simmer for about 20 minutes, until potatoes are very tender. Remove from heat and allow to cool.

• Mash the potatoes with a fork or force through a strainer and mix back into the broth. Add the peppers and salt and pepper to taste. Chill thoroughly in the refrigerator before serving.

Serves 4
Preparation time: 40 minutes, plus
chilling time.

Fried Poblano Pepper Rings with Avocado Dip

1 ripe avocado
juice of 1 lime
¼ cup sour cream
3 cups vegetable oil
1 cup all-purpose flour
1 teaspoon salt
1 teaspoon ground black pepper
3 poblano peppers cut into ¼-inch rings,
seeds removed
1 cup buttermilk

- To make the dip, peel the avocado and remove the pit. Place avocado in a bowl and mash with a fork. Add lime juice and sour cream and mix until smooth. Refrigerate until needed.
- Put the oil in a 2-quart saucepan and place over medium-high heat. Heat oil until just below the smoking point. If it begins to smoke, remove from heat, lower heat slightly, and replace. Take precautions for cooking with hot oil!
- Mix flour with salt and pepper and put on a plate. Coat a pepper ring with flour and shake off any excess. Dip into the buttermilk and then back into the flour. Drop carefully into the hot oil and cook until lightly browned. Repeat with the rest of the pepper rings. Do not crowd the pan—fry only 3 or 4 rings at a time. Remove fried pepper rings to paper towels to drain and keep warm.

Serves 4 to 6.
Preparation time: 45 minutes.

Crab and Pasilla Pepper Stuffed Eggs

12 hard-boiled eggs
1 dried pasilla pepper, soaked in hot
water for 30 minutes, seeded and
chopped
4–5 leaves fresh tarragon, minced, or
¼ teaspoon dried
¼ pound fresh crabmeat, cleaned
3 tablespoons mayonnaise
2 tablespoons Dijon mustard

• Cut eggs in half lengthwise. Remove
yolks to a bowl and set whites aside.
• Add chopped pepper, tarragon, crabmeat, mayonnaise and mustard to yolks
and mash together with a fork.
• Fill whites with yolk mixture using a
pastry bag or spoon.

Makes 24 pieces.
Preparation time: 45 minutes.

Seafood Stew with New Mexico Peppers

1 tablespoon vegetable oil
1 small onion, diced
2 fresh red or green New Mexico
peppers, seeded and chopped
6 mussels, scrubbed clean
6 clams, scrubbed clean
2 10-ounce cans thin unsweetened
coconut milk
1 scallion, coarsely chopped
6 large shrimp, peeled and deveined

- Place oil in a 2-quart saucepan over medium heat. Add the onion and peppers and sauté until wilted, about 5 minutes.
- Add the mussels, clams, coconut milk and scallion. Bring to a boil, then lower to a simmer. Add the shrimp; cover and cook for a few minutes, until the clams and mussels open. (Discard any unopened clams or mussels.)

Serves 2.
Preparation time: 45 minutes.

Note: Canned coconut milk can be obtained from shops specializing in Asian or Latin American groceries.

Monkfish with Roasted Cherry Peppers and Eggplant

6 pickled cherry peppers (or fresh if available)
¼ cup plus 2 tablespoons olive oil
1 small eggplant, peeled and cut into ½-inch cubes
2 cloves garlic, thinly sliced
2 sprigs fresh oregano, chopped, or 1 teaspoon dried
salt and pepper
1 pound monkfish fillet, cut into ¼-inch-thick medallions
¼ cup all-purpose flour

• Preheat oven to 350°.
• Place the peppers in a shallow baking pan and roast in the oven, turning occasionally, until the skin darkens and separates, about 20 to 30 minutes. Put peppers and any accumulated liquids in a bowl and cover until cooled. Peel and seed the peppers, reserving liquids in the bowl. Chop the peeled peppers coarsely and return them to the bowl.
• Heat ¼ cup olive oil in a skillet over medium heat. Add the eggplant, garlic, peppers and their juices, oregano and salt and pepper to taste. Lower heat and sauté until eggplant is cooked, about 5 minutes. Keep mixture warm.
• Heat 2 tablespoons of olive oil in a separate skillet over medium-high heat. Lightly dust the monkfish medallions with flour and sauté until brown on both sides and cooked throughout, about 3 to 5 minutes. Drain fish slices on paper towels and serve topped with the pepper-eggplant mixture.

Serves 4.
Preparation time: 1 hour 15 minutes.

Pork Chops with Ancho Pepper Sauce

2 tablespoons vegetable oil
4 large center-cut pork chops
1 medium-sized onion, chopped
2 cloves garlic, sliced
4 ancho peppers soaked in hot water for
30 minutes
1 tablespoon ground cumin
¼ cup white vinegar
juice of 1 orange
¼ cup chicken broth
3 tablespoons dark brown sugar
3 tablespoons ketchup

• Preheat oven to 350°.
• Heat 1 tablespoon of the oil in a large ovenproof skillet and brown the pork chops well on both sides. Put the skillet with the chops in the oven to finish cooking, about 10 to 15 minutes.
• While the pork chops are cooking, heat the remaining oil in a skillet over medium heat. Sauté the onion and garlic until wilted, about 5 minutes. Add the peppers, vinegar, orange juice, broth and brown sugar. Bring to a boil and cook for 1 minute. Add the ketchup, reduce heat and simmer until peppers are very soft, about 10 minutes.
• Puree the entire mixture in a blender or force through a sieve. Serve with the pork chops.

Serves 4.
Preparation time: 45 minutes.

Poblano Peppers with Beef and Olive Stuffing

8 poblano peppers
1 tablespoon vegetable oil
4–5 shallots, chopped
2 cloves garlic, thinly sliced
1 pound stewing beef, cut into ½-inch chunks
10 ounces chicken broth
16 green olives, pitted and halved
2 tablespoons capers
2 tablespoons paprika

- Cut the tops off the peppers and remove and discard the seeds and ribs. Set the hollowed-out peppers aside. Cut the stems out of the tops and chop the remaining pieces of pepper.
- Heat the oil in a medium-sized saucepan over medium heat. Add the chopped pepper, shallots and garlic and sauté until wilted, about 5 minutes. Remove from pan and set aside.
- Place the beef in the saucepan and brown well on all sides. Drain the liquid and return the sautéed pepper mixture to the pan. Add the chicken broth, olives, capers and paprika and bring to a boil. Lower to a simmer and cook until liquid is reduced and beef is tender.
- Bring a large pot of water to a boil. Cook the pepper shells in the boiling water for about 2 to 3 minutes—just until heated throughout and beginning to soften, but not so much that the peppers begin to lose their shape.
- Fill the cooked peppers with the hot beef mixture and serve.

Serves 4.
Preparation time: 1 hour 30 minutes.

Corn and Cherry Pepper Relish

1 12-ounce can water-packed corn,
drained
4 pickled cherry peppers, seeded and
diced
2 scallions, chopped
whites of 2 hard-boiled eggs, diced
¼ cup rice wine vinegar
2 tablespoons vegetable oil

• Combine corn, peppers, scallions and
chopped egg whites in a bowl.
• Whisk together vinegar and oil and pour
over relish. Allow to marinate for 1 hour
before serving.

Serves 4.
Preparation time: 10 minutes, plus
1 hour marinating time.

Pineapple with Ancho Pepper in Rum

2 ancho peppers, soaked in strong, hot tea for 30 minutes
6 ounces good-quality rum
1 fresh pineapple, peeled, cored and sliced

- Place the soaked peppers into the rum and allow to steep at least overnight (longer is better!).
- To serve, place the pineapple slices on a platter or on individual plates, and top with the rum.

Serves 4 to 6.
Preparation time: 35 minutes, set overnight, plus 10 minutes.

Walnut and New Mexico Pepper Tarts

Pastry

1½ cups all-purpose flour
¼ cup sugar
6 ounces cold unsalted butter, cut into small pieces
2 red New Mexico peppers, seeded and diced

Filling

8 ounces almond paste
3 egg yolks
¾ cup sugar
6 ounces unsalted butter, softened
¼ pound shelled walnuts, coarsely chopped

- Preheat oven to 350°.
- Combine flour and sugar for pastry. With your hands or a pastry cutter, work the cold butter into the flour mixture until it has the consistency of coarse cornmeal. Mix in the peppers. Sprinkle 3 to 4 tablespoons of very cold water on the dough and mix gently— add just enough water for dough to hold together in a ball. Wrap in plastic and refrigerate for 30 minutes.
- While the pastry dough is chilling, combine the almond paste, egg yolks, sugar and butter for the filling in a blender or food processor, and blend until smooth.
- Roll out the dough and press into six 5-inch round tart shells. Fill each with almond-paste mixture and top with walnuts. Place the tarts on a sheet pan and bake for 20 minutes or until the pastry is golden. Allow to cool before serving.

Serves 6.
Preparation time: 1 hour 15 minutes.

Peperoncini Martinis

4 pickled peperoncini peppers
1 ounce dry white vermouth
1 pint vodka

• Put 1 whole pepper into each of 4 large martini glasses. Fill a cocktail shaker with ice and add the vermouth. Swirl the vermouth around in the shaker and pour out the excess. Add the vodka, stir and strain into the glasses.

Serves 4.
Preparation time: 5 minutes.

MEDIUM

Jalapeño and Ham Corn Muffins

1½ cups yellow cornmeal
1½ cups all-purpose flour
2 tablespoons baking powder
¾ cup sugar
½ teaspoon salt
2 eggs
¾ cup milk
¼ cup vegetable oil
3 tablespoons honey
6 jalapeño peppers, seeded and diced
¼ pound ham, diced

• Preheat oven to 350°.
• Combine cornmeal, flour, baking powder, sugar and salt in a large bowl.
• Whisk together the eggs, milk, oil and honey. Pour into the dry-ingredient mixture and stir until completely combined. Stir in the diced peppers and ham.
• Pour the batter evenly into the cups of 1 12- or 2 6-muffin nonstick muffin tins. Bake for 8 minutes or until a toothpick inserted in the center of a muffin comes out clean.

Makes 12 muffins.
Preparation time: 20 minutes.

Scrambled Eggs with Wax Peppers and Okra

2 tablespoons unsalted butter
2 scallions, chopped
8–10 fresh okras, trimmed and cut into
¼-inch rounds
2 wax peppers, seeded and chopped
8 eggs, lightly beaten with 4 tablespoons
water

• Melt butter in a large skillet over medium heat. Add the scallions, okra and peppers and sauté until tender, about 5 to 10 minutes.
• Add the beaten eggs, lower heat and cook, stirring occasionally with a spatula, until desired doneness.

Serves 4.
Preparation time: 20 minutes.

Tomato and Wax Pepper Bisque

½ cup vegetable oil
½ cup flour
1 small onion, chopped
2 wax peppers, seeded and chopped
3 10-ounce cans crushed tomatoes in
puree
1 cup milk
1 tablespoon sugar
1 teaspoon dried thyme
1 teaspoon granulated garlic
salt and pepper
4 wax peppers, seeded

• Heat the oil in a large saucepan over medium heat. Whisk in the flour and continue stirring until the mixture is smooth and begins to brown slightly.
• Add the onion and chopped peppers and continue cooking until wilted, about 5 minutes. Add the tomatoes and their puree and bring to a boil, stirring.
• Stir in the milk, return to a low boil and reduce to a simmer. Add the sugar, thyme, garlic and salt and pepper to taste, and continue cooking for another 10 minutes.
• Bring 1 quart of water to a full boil and add the 4 seeded peppers. Cook until tender, about 5 minutes. Remove peppers and puree them in a blender or food processor.
• Pour the bisque into 4 bowls. Place a generous dollop of wax pepper puree into the center of each bowl and swirl the puree into the soup with the tip of a knife or a chopstick.

Serves 4.
Preparation time: 45 minutes.

Marinated White Bean and Chipotle Chili Salad

1 pound dry navy beans
¾ cup olive oil
¼ cup white wine vinegar
2 tablespoons Dijon mustard
4 chipotle chilies, soaked in hot water
for 20 minutes, seeded and julienned
2 scallions, chopped
2 sprigs fresh oregano, chopped, or
1 teaspoon dried
salt and pepper

- Wash beans and place in a large saucepan with 2 quarts of water. Bring to a boil and cook just until tender, about 1 hour. Be careful not to overcook the beans! Turn off the heat and allow the beans to cool in the water. Drain beans and place in a large bowl.
- Whisk together the oil, vinegar and mustard and pour over beans. Add the chilies, scallions and oregano. Salt and pepper to taste and mix well, taking care not to break the beans. Allow to marinate in the refrigerator, stirring occasionally, for at least 24 hours before serving.

Serves 8 to 10.
Preparation time: 2 hours, plus marinating time.

Shrimp with Guajillo Peppers and Basil

½ pound spaghetti or linguine
2 tablespoons olive oil
12 medium shrimp, peeled and deveined
4 cloves garlic, minced
2 guajillo peppers, soaked in hot water
for 30 minutes, seeded and julienned
1 ripe tomato, seeded and coarsely
chopped
10 green olives, pitted and halved
1–2 tablespoons capers
8–10 fresh basil leaves, cut into thin
strips

• Bring a large pot of salted water to a rapid boil and cook the pasta until *al dente*. Remove to a colander or strainer, cool under cold running water, toss with 1 tablespoon of olive oil and set aside. Bring a fresh pot of salted water to a rapid boil.

• While the second pot of water is heating, cook the shrimp: Place the remaining tablespoon of oil in a skillet over medium heat. Add the shrimp and garlic and sauté for 1 minute. Add the peppers, tomato, olives and capers and continue cooking just until the shrimp lose their translucence and begin to firm. Toss in the basil, cook for another minute and remove from heat.

• Place the cooked pasta in the fresh boiling water just long enough to reheat it—about a minute. Drain and divide between 2 plates. Top with the shrimp and serve.

Serves 2.
Preparation time: 45 minutes.

Stir-Fried Beef with Chipotle Chilies

1 pound skirt steak
¼ cup Worcestershire sauce
¼ cup Tabasco sauce
½ cup vegetable oil
1 tablespoon peanut oil
1 carrot, julienned
16 snow peas, julienned
¼ small head red cabbage, shredded
1 zucchini, coarsely chopped
4 chipotle chilies, finely ground or minced
¼ pound bean sprouts

• Trim meat of any fat and slice with the grain into finger-sized pieces.
• Mix Worcestershire sauce, Tabasco and vegetable oil in a bowl. Add the sliced steak, cover, and refrigerate overnight.
• Heat the peanut oil in a large skillet or wok over high heat. Add the carrot, snow peas, cabbage and zucchini and cook, stirring constantly, for about 2 minutes. Add the ground chilies and stir. Add the marinated steak pieces and continue stir-frying until just before meat reaches desired doneness. Add the bean sprouts, finish cooking and serve.

Serves 4.
Preparation time: 15 minutes, set overnight, plus 15 minutes.

Grilled Lamb with Guajillo Pepper and Spinach

½–¾ pound lamb (preferably from the leg), cut into 2-inch cubes
2 skewers
1 tablespoon olive oil
1 dried guajillo pepper, soaked in hot water for 30 minutes, seeded and julienned
1½ teaspoons ground cumin
½ teaspoon dried thyme
10 ounces fresh or frozen spinach (thawed and drained)
salt and pepper

• Preheat grill to high following manufacturer's instructions. (May be broiled if a grill is unavailable.) Skewer the lamb cubes and cook over the hottest spot on the grill to desired doneness.
• While the lamb is cooking, heat the olive oil in a skillet over medium heat. Add the pepper and sauté for about 3 or 4 minutes. Add the cumin and thyme and sauté for another minute. Add the spinach and cook just until hot. Add salt and pepper to taste.
• Arrange the spinach on 2 plates. When lamb is cooked, place on spinach mixture. Serve with rice, barley, couscous, pasta or potatoes.

Serves 2.
Preparation time: 45 minutes.

Flank Steak with Rocotillo Peppers and Garlic

4–5 cloves garlic, minced
1 flank steak, about 1½ pounds
salt and pepper
1 tablespoon vegetable oil
20 rocotillo peppers, whole or cut in
half, stems removed (remove seeds for
less heat)

- Rub the minced garlic mixed with salt and pepper to taste into both sides of the steak.
- Heat the oil in a large skillet over medium heat. Add the steak and lower heat to keep garlic from burning. Sauté steak on both sides to desired doneness, remove from pan, and slice diagonally against the grain. Place on plates or a serving platter.
- Add the peppers to the skillet and sauté over medium heat until tender, about 5 minutes. Arrange on sliced steak.

Serves 4.
Preparation time: 25 minutes.

Jalapeño Jelly

6–8 fresh jalapeño peppers, seeded and
chopped
2 cups white vinegar
½ cup sugar

• Place all ingredients in a nonreactive
saucepan and bring to a boil. Reduce to
low heat and simmer for about an hour,
until mixture is thick. Cool slightly and
puree in a blender or food processor.
• Pour into a jar and allow to cool completely. Cover and refrigerate overnight
before serving. Will keep for several
weeks in the refrigerator.

Makes about 1½ cups jelly.
Preparation time: 1 hour 15 minutes,
plus cooling time.

Chipotle Chili Oil and Vinegar

4 chipotle chilies, soaked in hot water
for 20 minutes
6 cloves garlic, peeled
1 pint extra-virgin olive oil
2 sprigs fresh rosemary
1 pint white wine vinegar
2 sprigs fresh thyme

• Place 2 chilies and 3 cloves of garlic into the bottle of olive oil. Add the rosemary and cap or cork tightly.

• Place 2 chilies and 3 cloves of garlic into the bottle of vinegar. Add the thyme and cap or cork tightly. Allow oil and vinegar to steep in a cool, dark place (not in the refrigerator) for at least 2 days, longer if possible. Both will keep for several months. Use for salads, marinating meats and vegetables, sautéing or in any recipe that calls for very flavorful oil or vinegar.

Makes 1 pint of oil and 1 pint of vinegar. Preparation time: 20 minutes, plus steeping time.

Candied Jalapeños

1½ cups sugar
10 jalapeño peppers with long stems

• Place the sugar and ½ cup water into a heavy-bottomed pan over medium-high heat. Bring to a boil, stirring to dissolve the sugar. Lower the heat to medium and continue cooking until the syrup temperature reaches the hard ball stage on a candy thermometer, about 250°. (If a thermometer is unavailable, test for the proper temperature by dropping a small amount of syrup into cold water. It is ready if it forms a hard ball.)
• Holding the pepper stems carefully with your fingers or small tongs, dip each pepper into the sugar syrup to coat it entirely. Place on wax paper to harden.

Makes 10 peppers.
Preparation time: 30 minutes.

Rocotillo Pepper and Coconut Sorbet

1 10-ounce can thin, unsweetened
coconut milk
juice of 2 limes
2 egg whites
8–10 rocotillo peppers, seeded and
chopped

• Combine all ingredients in an ice cream machine (minimum 1-quart capacity); process according to manufacturer's instructions and place in freezer to ripen.

Serves 4.
Preparation time: 30 minutes, plus freezing time.

Note: Canned coconut milk may be obtained from stores specializing in Latin American or Asian groceries.

Jalapeño Margaritas

4 jalapeño peppers, halved lengthwise
1 pint tequila
1 ounce Triple Sec liqueur
3 ounces bottled or fresh lime juice
coarse salt for garnish (optional)

• Put the peppers in the bottle of tequila and allow to steep for at least 3 days.

• For 4 margaritas, pour 5 ounces of jalapeño tequila, 1 ounce Triple Sec and 3 ounces lime juice into a cocktail shaker filled with ice. Stir and strain into glasses either straight up or over fresh ice cubes. (If desired, first dip the rims of the glasses into lime juice and then into salt.)

Serves 4.
Preparation time: Steeping time, plus 5 minutes.

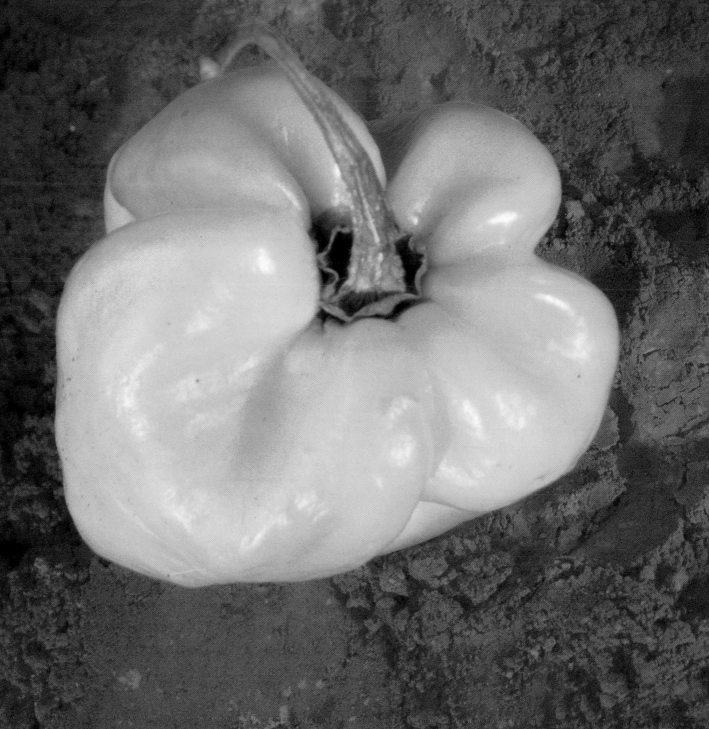

Cold Shrimp with Cayenne Mayonnaise

2 lemons, quartered
1 tablespoon black peppercorns
2 bay leaves
1 pound medium shrimp, shells on
2 egg yolks
1 tablespoon Dijon mustard
juice of 1 lemon
1½ cups olive oil
2 teaspoons ground cayenne pepper

• Place lemon pieces, peppercorns, bay leaves and 1 quart of water into a large saucepan. Bring to a boil, lower heat and simmer for 10 minutes. Add the shrimp and cook just until firm, about 3 to 4 minutes. Drain and set the shrimp aside to cool (discard the other solids). When shrimp is cool, peel, devein and refrigerate until chilled.

• Combine the egg yolks, mustard and lemon juice in a clean, dry bowl or the container of a food processor, whisking or processing briefly. Add the olive oil in a thin, steady stream, whisking or processing constantly until all of the oil has been used and the mayonnaise has formed. Stir in the cayenne, adjusting the amount to taste. Serve with the cold shrimp.

Serves 4.
Preparation time: 1 hour.

Baked Grits with Piquin Chilies and Cheese

1 cup grits
1 teaspoon salt
2 tablespoons unsalted butter
2 tablespoons piquin chilies, crushed
(use a blender or spice grinder)
3 egg yolks
¾ cup grated Parmesan cheese

- Preheat oven to 400°.
- Put grits, salt, butter and chilies into a saucepan and add 4 cups cold water. Bring to a boil, lower heat and simmer until grits are cooked, about 20 to 25 minutes. Remove from heat and let cool for about 10 minutes.
- Break up egg yolks in a bowl. Add a little of the warm grits and mix. Return the yolk and grits mixture to the pan and stir quickly. Mix in ½ cup of the cheese, pour mixture into a 9- × 12-inch baking pan and bake until firm, about 20 minutes. Top with the remaining cheese and place under the broiler for a few minutes, until lightly browned.

Serves 6.
Preparation time: 1 hour.

Fish Chowder with Habanero Peppers

1 tablespoon vegetable oil
1 celery stalk, thinly sliced
1 medium-sized onion, chopped
2 medium-sized waxy potatoes, cut into
½-inch chunks (skin optional)
1 pound catfish fillet, cut into large
pieces
2 tablespoons granulated garlic
2 tablespoons dried thyme
2 bay leaves
6 cups clam juice or fish stock
1 cup tomato paste
4–5 habanero peppers, left whole or cut
in half (remove seeds for less heat)
1 pound medium shrimp, peeled,
deveined and cut in half crosswise
salt and pepper

- Heat oil in a large saucepan over medium heat. Add the celery, onion and potatoes and sauté until tender, about 5 to 10 minutes. Add the fish and continue cooking for 2 to 3 minutes. Add the garlic, thyme and bay leaves.
- Add the clam juice or stock, tomato paste and peppers. Bring the soup to a boil, lower to a simmer and cook for 30 minutes. Add the shrimp and salt and pepper to taste. Continue cooking for about 2 minutes, just until the shrimp loses its translucence.

Serves 8.
Preparation time: 1 hour.

Warm Beef Salad with Thai Peppers

1 tablespoon vegetable oil
2 8-ounce filets mignons
¼ head Chinese cabbage, shredded
1 bunch watercress, coarsely torn
½ head Boston lettuce, coarsely torn
1 5-ounce can bamboo shoots, drained
1 5-ounce can baby corn, drained
¼ pound fresh bean sprouts
4 green or red Thai peppers, seeded and julienned
2 lemons, halved

• Heat the oil in a skillet over high heat until just below the smoking point. Add the steaks and sear on all sides. Lower the heat and continue cooking until desired doneness. Allow to cool until warm or room temperature.
• Toss together the cabbage, watercress and lettuce and arrange on 4 plates. Top with the bamboo shoots, baby corn, bean sprouts and peppers. Squeeze the juice of half a lemon over each.
• Slice the steaks and arrange a few pieces on top of each salad.

Serves 4.
Preparation time: 45 minutes.

Fried Chicken with Piquin Chili Breading

2 cups all-purpose flour
2–3 tablespoons piquin chilies, crushed
(use a blender or a spice grinder)
1 teaspoon salt
1 teaspoon ground black pepper
2 cups vegetable oil (peanut oil is best)
8 pieces chicken
2 cups buttermilk

• Combine flour, chilies and salt and pepper in a shallow bowl.

• Heat the oil in a deep saucepan until very hot. (The oil is hot enough if a little flour dropped in it starts to bubble and cook immediately.) Dip a piece of chicken into the flour mixture, coating all sides, then into the buttermilk and back into the flour. Carefully put it into the hot oil and repeat with 1 or 2 more pieces—do not crowd the pan. Cook chicken pieces until done and drain on paper towels. (To test for doneness, poke a knife into a piece of chicken—if the juices run clear, it is done.) Repeat with remaining chicken, cooking only 2 or 3 pieces at a time.

Serves 4.
Preparation time: 1 hour.

Pork Loin with Thai Pepper Butter

2 red or green Thai peppers, seeded and
sliced into thin rings
¼ pound unsalted butter, softened
salt and pepper
1 tablespoon vegetable oil
1 pork loin, tied, about 1½ pounds

- Preheat oven to 350°.
- Mix peppers into softened butter and add salt and pepper to taste. Place butter on a piece of foil, wax paper or plastic wrap in a log shape about 1½ inches in diameter and about 3 to 4 inches long. Roll wrapping around butter, smooth out the shape and refrigerate until firm. (Extra butter can be kept in the freezer for several weeks.)
- While the butter is chilling, heat the oil in a large, ovenproof skillet over medium heat. Add the tied pork loin and brown on all sides. Place the skillet in the oven and roast until pork is firm to the touch, about 40 minutes.
- Remove roast from oven, cut off strings, and slice pork. Slice the cold butter into ¼-inch-thick rounds and place one piece of butter on each serving of meat.

Serves 4.
Preparation time: 1 hour 30 minutes.

Arbol Chili con Carne

1 tablespoon vegetable oil
1 onion, chopped
1 green bell pepper, seeded and chopped
¾ pound ground beef
½ pound stewing beef, cut into ½-inch
cubes
1¼ cups chicken broth
3 whole dried arbol chilies
2 tablespoons ground cumin
2 tablespoons commercial chili powder
2 tablespoons granulated garlic
salt and pepper

• Heat oil in a large saucepan over medium heat. Add the onion and green bell
pepper and sauté until both are wilted,
about 5 minutes. Remove from pan and
set aside.
• Put the ground and cubed beef into the
saucepan and sauté until thoroughly
cooked, about 10 minutes. Drain off fat
and put cooked green pepper and onion
back in the pan with the beef.
• Add the chicken broth, arbol chilies, cumin, chili powder, garlic and salt and
pepper to taste. Simmer over medium-
low heat until most of the liquid has
evaporated, about 1 hour. Serve with
white beans or pasta, either combined
with the chili or on the side.

Serves 4.
Preparation time: 1 hour 30 minutes.

Habanero Pepper, Onion and Coriander Chutney

1 tablespoon vegetable oil
1 large onion, cut in half and sliced into half rings
6 habanero peppers, coarsely chopped (remove the seeds and ribs for less heat)
zest of 1 orange, julienned
6 pitted prunes, coarsely chopped
2 large sprigs fresh coriander, leaves removed from stems and set aside
¼ cup sugar
¼ cup rum

- Heat oil in a medium-sized saucepan over medium heat; add the onion and sauté until wilted, about 5 minutes. Add the peppers, orange zest, prunes and coriander stems. Sauté for 3 or 4 minutes.
- Add just enough water to cover the mixture and stir in the sugar. Bring to a boil, lower heat to medium and cook for about 10 minutes, until liquid is reduced. Allow to cool slightly, remove the coriander stems, and stir in the coriander leaves and rum. Refrigerate when completely cooled.

Makes about 1½ cups chutney.
Preparation time: 30 minutes, plus chilling time.

Habanero Hot Sauce

10 habanero peppers, minced (seeds optional)
¼ cup cider vinegar
1 teaspoon salt
1 tablespoon sugar

- Combine all ingredients in a bowl or jar. Will keep in the refrigerator, covered, for several weeks.

Makes ¾ cup sauce.
Preparation time: 15 minutes.

Serrano-Ginger Custard

4 eggs
1 cup sugar
2 tablespoons orange liqueur
1 tablespoon fresh ginger, peeled and
minced
3 red or green serrano peppers, seeded
and diced
1 quart heavy cream

• Whisk together eggs and sugar in the top of a double boiler or a flameproof glass bowl. Add the liqueur, ginger, peppers and cream.
• Place the bowl over (not in!) simmering water and cook, stirring constantly, until mixture thickens, about 30 minutes. Pour into serving bowls and refrigerate until firm, about 2 hours.

Serves 8.
Preparation time: 45 minutes, plus chilling time.

Mangoes with Cayenne and Crenshaw Sauce

2 mangoes, sliced
½ crenshaw melon, peeled, seeded and diced
2 dried cayenne peppers, crushed (seeds optional)

• Arrange mango pieces on 4 plates.
• Put the diced melon and crushed peppers in a saucepan over high heat. Bring to a boil and cook for 1 or 2 minutes. Remove from heat and spoon the hot sauce over the mango slices.

Serves 4 to 6.
Preparation time: 15 minutes.

Serrano Rum

1 750-ml bottle good-quality dark rum
2–3 cinnamon sticks
1 vanilla bean, split in half lengthwise
3 whole cloves
6–8 serrano peppers, cut in half
lengthwise and seeded

• Place all ingredients in the bottle with the rum and allow to steep for at least 1 week. (You may need to pour out a bit of the rum to make room for the solids.) The flavor improves with age—it will keep for months.

Makes about 700 ml.
Preparation time: 5 minutes, plus steeping time.

RECEIPE LIST ◆◀◀◀◀◀◆

RECEIPE LIST BY PEPPER ◆▶▶▶▶▶◆

Ancho
Pineapple with Ancho Pepper
   in Rum · 62
Pork Chops with Ancho Pepper
   Sauce · 56

Arbol
Arbol Chili con Carne · 108

Bell
Bell Pepper Confetti Pizza · 30
Green Bell Pepper and Bacon
   Frittata · 18
Marinated Bell Pepper and Mushroom
   Relish · 34
Red Bell Pepper and Tomato Juice · 38
Roasted Red Bell Pepper and Green
   Bean Salad · 26
Roasted Yellow Bell Pepper Soup · 22
Scallop and Yellow Bell Pepper
   Skewers · 24

Cayenne
Cold Shrimp with Cayenne
   Mayonnaise · 96
Mangoes with Cayenne and Crenshaw
   Sauce · 114

Cherry
Corn and Cherry Pepper Relish · 60
Monkfish with Roasted Cherry Peppers
   and Eggplant · 54

Chipotle
Chipotle Chili Oil and Vinegar · 88
Marinated White Bean and Chipotle
   Chili Salad · 76
Stir-Fried Beef with Chipotle Chilies · 80

Guajillo
Grilled Lamb with Guajillo Pepper and
   Spinach · 82
Shrimp with Guajillo Peppers and
   Basil · 78

Habanero
Fish Chowder with Habanero
   Peppers · 100
Habanero Hot Sauce · 110
Habanero Pepper, Onion and Coriander
   Chutney · 110

Jalapeño
Candied Jalapeños · 90
Jalapeño and Ham Corn Muffins · 70
Jalapeño Jelly · 86
Jalapeño Margaritas · 92

New Mexico
Salmon with New Mexico Pepper and
   Lime · 44
Seafood Stew with New Mexico
   Peppers · 52
Walnut and New Mexico Pepper
   Tarts · 64

Pasilla
Cold Potato and Pasilla Pepper Soup · 46
Crab and Pasilla Pepper Stuffed
   Eggs · 50

Peperoncini
Peperoncini and Roast Beef Hash · 42
Peperoncini Martinis · 66

Piquin
Baked Grits with Piquin Chilies and
   Cheese · 98
Fried Chicken with Piquin Chili
   Breading · 104

Poblano
Fried Poblano Pepper Rings with
   Avocado Dip · 48
Poblano Peppers with Beef and Olive
   Stuffing · 58

Rocotillo
Flank Steak with Rocotillo Peppers and
   Garlic · 84
Rocotillo Pepper and Coconut
   Sorbet · 90

Serrano
Serrano Rum · 116
Serrano-Ginger Custard · 112

Sweet Italian
Pickled Sweet Italian Peppers, Carrots
   and Cauliflower · 36
Sweet Italian Pepper and Onion
   Bread · 20
Sweet Italian Peppers with Chicken and
   Pignoli Stuffing · 28
Veal Rolls with Sweet Italian Pepper
   Filling · 32

Thai
Pork Loin with Thai Pepper Butter · 106
Warm Beef Salad with Thai
   Peppers · 102

Wax
Scrambled Eggs with Wax Peppers and
   Okra · 72
Tomato and Wax Pepper Bisque · 74

SOURCES ◆◀◀◀◀◀◆

Cascados Farms
PO Box 1269
San Juan Pueblo, NM 87566
Whole, ground and crushed dried chilies;
chili ristras. Write for catalogue.

Creole Delicacies Company Inc.
533 St. Ann Street
New Orleans, LA 80116
(504) 525-9508
Pepper relishes and hot Cajun spice mixes;
call or write for catalogue.

Dean & DeLuca
Mail Order Department
560 Broadway
New York, NY 10012
(800) 221-7714
(212) 431-1691 in NY
Dried and pickled peppers; call or write for
catalogue ($2.00).

Desert Rose Salsa Company
PO Box 5391
Tucson, AZ 85703
(602) 743-0450
Marinated cherry peppers, prepared salsas;
call or write for price list.

DeWildt Imports, Inc.
(800) 338-3433
Wide variety of sambals (Indonesian chili
paste) and chili-based sauces; call for
catalogue.

The El Paso Chile Company
100 Ruhlin Court
El Paso, TX 79922
(915) 544-3434
Dried and canned chilies; chili wreaths and
ristras; prepared sauces and salsas. Call or
write for catalogue.

Gourmet Treasure Hunters
10044 Adams Avenue, Suite 305
Huntington Beach, CA 92646
(714) 964-3355
Wide range of American regional and
international ingredients including a
hot pepper sauce called Tennessee Sunshine
and canned coconut milk. Call or write
for subscription to catalogue and
newsletter ($4.00).

Los Chileros de Nueva Mexico
PO Box 6215
Santa Fe, NM 87502
(505) 471-6967
Wide range of dried chilies; chili ristras and
wreaths. Call or write for price list.

Melissa's Brand
World Variety Produce
PO Box 21127
Los Angeles, CA 90021
(800) 468-7111
(213) 588-0151 in CA
Large selection of fresh and dried peppers by
mail; call to check availability.

Native Seeds/SEARCH
2509 North Campbell Avenue, #325
Tucson, AZ 85719
(602) 327-9123
Hot pepper seeds for gardeners from this
non-profit group dedicated to preserving
native southwestern American crops; call or
write for catalogue ($1.00).

Pendery's Inc.
304 East Belknap Street
Fort Worth, TX 76102
(800) 533-1870
Wide variety of dried whole and ground
chilies; chili ristras and wreaths; chili-printed
gift wrap. Call or write for catalogue.

The Pepper Gal
10536 119th Avenue North
Largo, FL 34643
Large variety of hot, sweet and ornamental
pepper seeds for gardeners; write for
catalogue.

R&R Mill Company, Inc.
Smithfield Implement Company
45 West First North
Smithfield, VT 84335
(801) 563-3333
Food dehydrators for making your own dried
peppers.

G.B. Ratto & Company
821 Washington Street
Oakland, CA 94607
(800) 325-3483
(800) 228-3515 in CA
Wide range of dried whole and ground
chilies; call or write for catalogue.

Spice Merchant
PO Box 524
Jackson Hole, WY 83001
(307) 733-7811
Wide variety of dried whole and ground
chilies; call or write for catalogue.

Tomato Growers Supply Company
PO Box 2237
Fort Myers, FL 33902
(813) 768-1119
A variety of hot and sweet pepper seeds for
gardeners; call or write for catalogue.

Chris Weeks Peppers
PO Box 3207
Kill Devil Hills, NC 27948
Many exotic hot pepper seeds for gardeners;
send self-addressed stamped envelope for
catalogue.